WELCOME TO STANI

Stanley Mills were founded ov by a group of Perth merchants, with technical and financial support from Richard Arkwright, the 'father' of the English cotton industry. The Bell Mill, the original cotton mill, is probably the best surviving example of an Arkwright-designed mill anywhere in the world.

Textiles were manufactured here almost continuously from 1787 until 1989. As demands changed and technologies developed, buildings were added, adapted, expanded, destroyed by fire, rebuilt, shut down, reopened and demolished. Machinery came and went, powered initially by water wheels, and latterly by electricity generated by water-powered turbines on the site.

It is now possible to explore the buildings and discover the many changes that took place over two centuries.

Above: The Bell Mill's distinctive round window, belfry and spire.

Opposite: A view of the mills from the west during restoration. The weaving shed visible adjacent to the Bell Mill has now been demolished.

CONTENTS

STANLEY MILLS AT A GLANCE

Stanley Mills stand on a peninsula formed by a hairpin bend in the River Tay. The site is remote from west coast ports such as Port Glasgow, through which raw cotton was imported, and was established well before the arrival of the railway. It was chosen because of the tremendous water-power available here.

The Tay is the fastest-flowing river in the UK, and drops 6.5 metres (21ft) as it snakes around the peninsula. A tunnel had been driven through the peninsula as early as 1729, to power a corn mill. The cotton mill was built in 1786, at the beginning of the Industrial Revolution. The nearby village of Stanley was established around the same time, to provide accommodation for the workforce. Later expansion and adaptation at the mills are evident from the buildings arranged around the Mill Square, and in the surrounding area.

Opposite: The Mill Square, looking west towards the Bell Mill.

THE POWER OF WATER

THE MACHINE AGE

WORKING LIFE

LIFE ON THE TAY

A SHORT TOUR OF STANLEY MILLS

On this tour, you will visit the lade (artificial watercourse), the Gatehouse, the Bell Mill, the Wheel Pits, part of the Mid Mill and some of the other buildings around the Mill Square, as well as the Turbine House, built in 1921 to provide electricity for the machinery.

The East Mill and part of the Mid Mill are now private housing, converted by the Phoenix Trust with financial support from the Heritage Lottery Fund. Please respect the privacy of the residents. Please also be aware that the peninsula beyond the mills is private property.

This tour will help you understand the process of cotton production and the supply of water-power. It will also provide some insights into the working lives of the employees. You may also like to explore nearby Stanley village, which was built to house the mill workers.

Illustration key

1. Car park
2. Gatehouse
3. Corn Mill
4. Bell Mill
5. Wheel Pits
6. Mid Mill
7. East Mill
8. East Range
9. North Range
10. Turbine House

OUTSIDE THE MILLS

THE LADE

From the car park, a walkway leads to the mills along the lade, or canal, which supplied the water-power for Stanley Mills. This system was designed by the Duke of Atholl's factor, James Stobie, in 1785.

He engineered a new tunnel to divert part of the river through the hill, replacing the corn mill tunnel of 1729. Stobie's tunnel is 237m long but drops just 41cm in height, emerging into the lade to feed the water wheels that once powered the Bell Mill.

When Buchanan & Co. of Glasgow took over the mills in 1823, they installed a third tunnel 244m long, arched and paved throughout. This gave an improved fall of almost 5m and drove no fewer than seven water wheels, generating some 200 horsepower.

THE GATEHOUSE

The circular gatehouse was probably constructed during the Buchanan expansion programme of 1823–5. A single-storey, stone-built lodge with a fine ogee slate roof, it was used to check workers and visitors in and out of the mills. The Gatehouse now acts as an orientation point for the site.

THE MILL SQUARE

The mill buildings are arranged around the Mill Square. At its centre is the gasworks chimney. Originally 36.5m tall, it was later reduced to its current height of 26m. Before the gasworks were built around 1825, the mills were lit by candles, which brought a great risk of fire. In front of the chimney are the footings of a gasometer, in which gas was stored (see photograph, page 26).

Nearest to the Gatehouse is the Bell Mill, the original cotton mill. In the centre is the Mid Mill, and on the far side, the East Mill. Opposite the Mid Mill, flanking the lade, is the North Range, which once housed office buildings and the cigarette tape-weaving department.

THE CORN MILL

Just to the west of the Bell Mill is the site of the water-powered corn mill, built in 1729. Evidence of gable ends, doors, windows and other features is visible on the Bell Mill wall, but these belong to a weaving shed erected after the corn mill was demolished. From here, the powerful Tay can be viewed.

Above: The Mill Square, looking down from the East Mill.

Opposite: The North Lade runs under the main entrance to the Mill Square.

Below: The site of the former corn mill, built in the 1720s.

7

THE BELL MILL

LEVEL I: 200 YEARS OF COTTON PRODUCTION

Built in 1786–7, the Bell Mill is the oldest building on the site. It is a rare surviving example of a cotton mill from the early industrial period. The Bell Mill originally had four upper storeys, built of locally made brick, with a stone-built ground floor and basement. This is an early use of brick in Perthshire and shows the influence of Arkwright's Derbyshire mills on the design.

Halfway up the walls of the ground floor, there is evidence of a floor that has been removed. This change was probably made in the early 20th century, when more height was needed to accommodate large looms. The cast iron supporting columns are hollow and cylindrical, whereas the older columns on the floors above are solid and cruciform.

BELL MILL, LEVEL 0: TAR TANK

This outhouse was added in the late 19th century, and has changed very little since then. The tank was used to steep cotton belting in tar, to waterproof it for industrial use. Tarred belting – used to drive machinery – was one of the chief products made here from the 1880s to the 1960s. It was sold throughout the world and helped sustain the mills as a profitable business.

BELL MILL, LEVEL 0:
THE ARCHAEOLOGY OF POWER

From 1787 until larger wheel-pits were built around 1823, this area housed the mechanisms that transmitted power from the water wheel to the machinery. The factory's main drive-shaft ran through the trench underfoot.

The drive-shaft was connected to the machines by a system of gears, shafts and belts. Line shafts ran along the ceilings of the factory, and were connected to each machine via a belt. In this way, mechanical power was distributed throughout the factory.

The deep window bays housed the mill's first heating stoves. Cotton had to be spun at high temperatures and the spinning mill was heated to 18–23°C (65–74°F). On one pillar you can make out an indentation in the plaster. This was once part of a system of flues to carry heat around the building.

At the far end of this room you can see a valve from the sprinkler system, which was installed in the late 19th century. Cotton fibre is highly flammable and many mills burned down.

Above: The Bell Mill basement, which housed machinery to transfer power from the water wheel to the machines.

Opposite: The Bell Mill has changed little since it was built in the 1780s.

Below: This indentation marks a point where there was once a hole in the masonry. It was part of a system of flues designed to carry warm air around the factory.

THE WHEEL PITS

Just outside the basement are a pair of wheel pits on the site of the Bell Mill's original wheel. They date from Buchanan & Co.'s expansion of 1823–5. The wheel pits have been adapted many times. At different points in the mill's development, the pits held at least three different configurations of wheels. A pair of wheel pits still lies on the eastern side of Mill Square, but has not been excavated.

In 1879, a 'Jonval' turbine by Thomson & Co. of Dundee was installed in the wheel pits to power the machinery. A second turbine was later added in the eastern wheel pits. From the 1820s until the early 20th century, the mills were lit by gas. In 1908, a Gilkes water turbine was installed to generate electricity for lighting. You can still see the concrete casing that secured it in place.

Above: The sluice-gate mechanism above the Wheel Pits was used to control flow of water onto the wheels.

Left: The twin Wheel Pits seen here were installed in the 1820s.

This heavy engineering was designed to withstand the enormous power of the water – but it weakened over time. The circular grooves on the pit wall were formed when the 6m-diameter wheel became unbalanced. You can also see evidence of shattered masonry, caused by vibration in the wheel bearings. The masonry was replaced with timber, which absorbed vibration better, but has since rotted away.

The wheel pits were eventually filled in and forgotten. They were rediscovered after Historic Scotland acquired the site.

HOW THE MACHINES WERE USED

Carding machine made by Philipson & Co. during the 1950s. These machines were used to process rolls of cotton fibres into long, fat ropes called 'slivers' or 'slubbing'. The slivers were then stretched on drawing machines until they became thin enough to spin. *See it in the Mid Mill, Level 2*

Spinner developed at Stanley Mills around 1970. Machines of this kind were used on the attic floor of the East Mill. The motor was adapted from a car dynamo. *See it in the Bell Mill, Level 1*

Tape weaving loom operated by women in the North Range Banding Room from 1916 until 1976. These machines were used to produce narrow cotton tape for the manufacture of cigarettes and cigars (see pages 16–17). The width of the tape was measured precisely, using a specially designed gauge. *See it in the Bell Mill, Level 1*

Calender rolling machine used to smooth the surface of cotton tape as part of the finishing process. Heavy heated rollers were used to flatten the tapes. Wax could then be applied to provide a further smoothness. *See it in the Bell Mill, Level 1*

THE MID MILL

The Mid Mill was built in two stages. The main part was constructed in 1823–5, during the Buchanan expansion programme. It was used for carding, spinning and weaving cotton, so fireproofing was an important consideration. It was built from stone, with iron beams, cast-iron columns and vaulted brick floors rather than wooden ceilings.

The Mid Mill was extended at both ends around 1830–40, connecting it to the Bell Mill and the East Mill. From the exterior you can see variations in the masonry at the points where the original building was extended. It was originally four storeys with attics – though one storey was later removed. You can see the outline of the earlier roof in the Bell Mill's stair tower. At the ground-level entrance to the carding room you can see curved channels cut into the walls around the doorway. These were made by mill engineers: it was the only way they could install the large main drums of the carding machines you see in this room.

Above: The Mid Mill seen from the other side of the Tay.

Left: One of the iron braces used to strengthen the structure.

Below: The ground-level entrance to the carding room.

LEVEL I: CARDING ROOM

The machines in this room date from the 1950s. They are the only cotton machines in Scotland that are still in their original positions. These four carding machines were built by Philipson & Co. of Bolton, Lancashire.

Carding was originally a manual process performed with a 'card' – a flat wooden block fitted with rows of angled spikes and a handle. This was used to comb out raw cotton into strips known as 'slivers'. Carding later became a mechanised process, which was less arduous but filled the air with cotton fibre.

The noise of the machines also made normal conversation impossible, so workers at Stanley and other textile factories in Dundee, Paisley and Lancashire developed a system of sign language. It was used to convey simple messages like the time of day, but also for more subversive purposes, such as early warning of the presence of the foreman.

Willie Whyte, who worked at Stanley in the 1960s, remembers the 'kinda fierce women' who worked in the card room. 'They were onto hand signals,' he recalls. 'I don't know what they were saying.'

'It was horrible. I got a cough never gone away yet. I went away from the factory because bad for my health.'

Italian-born Lena Wasinovicz, who worked in the carding room 1954–6.

Below: This detail from a 19th-century print shows women and young girls working in a carding room. The shaft and belts driving the machines can be seen above their heads.

BELL MILL, LEVEL 2: THE ARKWRIGHT MILL

The upper floor of the Bell Mill has hardly changed since it first opened in 1787. In fact, it is one of the best-preserved 18th-century workspaces anywhere in the world.

It was designed by the cotton spinner Richard Arkwright to house the water-powered carding and spinning frames for which he held a patent. Many original features have survived, such as the heating system and the large windows, designed to let light in during long working days.

The cast-iron columns were probably inserted in the first couple of decades after the Bell Mill's construction, enabling the floors to take the weight of heavier machinery.

The workers would have been mainly women and children, recruited from all over Perthshire – both the Gaelic-speaking Highland areas and the English/Scots-speaking Lowlands. Later on, orphans from the Perth workhouse came to work at the mills.

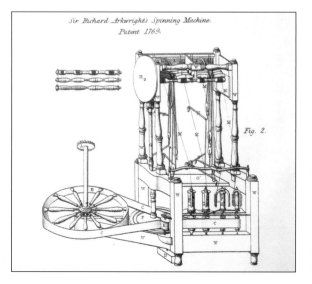

Above: Arkwright's design, including many large windows, was based on his earlier cotton mills in the North and Midlands of England.

Left: Arkwright's patent spinning frame, turned from a wheel set on a vertical axle, which could be powered by a horse or by water.

SIR RICHARD ARKWRIGHT

Richard Arkwright was born in 1732 at Preston, Lancashire, the youngest of seven children. He trained as a barber and became a successful wigmaker, pioneering the use of hair dye; and later became an innkeeper.

In 1767 he employed a clockmaker, John Kay, with whom he developed a cotton-spinning machine. An associate of Kay, Thomas Highs, claimed the design had been stolen from him, but it was Arkwright who won a patent for the machine, in July 1769.

With several business partners he established a horse-powered mill in Nottingham. He later developed a water-powered version, the 'water frame', and in 1771 opened the first water-powered cotton mill at Cromford in Derbyshire.

His business interests in the North of England expanded and in 1775 he took out a further patent, embracing the whole cotton-spinning process. He used this to pursue lawsuits against competitors, but not all were successful. In 1785 his patent was challenged by a Crown prosecution and revoked.

Nonetheless, he enjoyed some popularity. In 1784, he visited Glasgow, where he was feted as 'the ingenious manufacturer of cotton-yarn' and presented with the freedom of the city. He received the same honour in Perth, and when he was knighted in 1786, his sponsors included George Dempster, MP for the Perth Burghs, who was a partner at Stanley.

He took a paternalistic approach to employment, allowing his workers some holidays and throwing annual feasts for them, but placing strict restraints on their freedom.

Many considered his business practices unscrupulous, but by the time of his death in 1792 he was one of the richest men in Britain.

AROUND THE MILL SQUARE

THE EAST MILL

The original East Mill was built in the 1790s, not long after the Bell Mill. It was used for processing flax to make linen yarn, but burned down in 1799. It was repaired and reopened around 1802, then extended in 1823–5. Today, the building has seven storeys including basement and attics. It has its own internal wheel-pit, but the layout suggests that mule-spinning may also have been carried out here.

By the 1980s, this building was used to spin acrylic fibres. It is now occupied by private housing.

Above: The Mill Square, with the North Range to the left and the East Mill to the right.

THE NORTH RANGE

On the northern edge of the Mill Square stands a range of stone-built buildings dating from 1823 to 1852. These buildings held the company offices and other departments. A later single-storey building once stood at the centre of the range, where one of the lades passes underfoot. It was used at different times for tape looms and knitwear machinery.

From 1916, these buildings housed machinery for making cigarette tape. This was a 2cm-wide 'endless' cotton belt, used in the manufacure of cigarettes. The tape formed a cradle in which tobacco and paper were conveyed through the production process.

Cigarettes were not manufactured here at Stanley, but the tape became a commercially important product for the mills. It was produced in conditions of great secrecy for fear of industrial espionage.

At the eastern end of the North Range stands a small building in the neo-Gothic style. This was the gatehouse to Stanley Estate. Marks left by the gate's hinges can be seen on the adjoining wall.

THE EAST RANGE

Behind the East Mill is a warehouse, built between 1823 and 1840, where raw cotton was stored before spinning. The warehouse runs into a two-storey weaving block from the same period, possibly used originally for handlooms. Behind that is the bleaching department, dating from the same period but extended later. By 1912, it housed a stone bleaching croft, a brick-built chlorine house and a stone-and-brick drying house.

'We were called "the snobs" – maybe because it was a cleaner environment. They used to come out of the mill with the cotton and everything sticking in their hair.'

Margaret Reiche, who worked in the cigarette tape department in the 1940s.

RIVER DWELLERS

This stretch of the Tay is abundant with Atlantic salmon. In the early days of Stanley Mills, sponsors such as David Dale and Robert Owen received gifts of fresh salmon.

Also plentiful are brook lamprey (right), sea lamprey and river lamprey. Although they resemble eels, lampreys are not strictly fish: fossil evidence shows that they have existed for at least 450 million years. The mouth is a sucker lined with teeth. Sea and river lamprey are parasites which attach themselves to other marine species, feeding off their flesh.

Birds present here include goosander and red-breasted merganser. These handsome diving ducks belong to the sawbill family, so called because of their long, serrated bills, used for catching fish.

There are also otters in the area. These secretive, playful mammals were hunted until the 1950s, but it was the insecticide DDT that nearly eradicated them. Thankfully, numbers are now rising.

THE WIDER LANDSCAPE

THE PENINSULA

To the east of the mills, a path takes you further into the peninsula formed by a tight bend in the River Tay at Stanley. From here, you can see the 1921 turbine house and the tunnels bringing the water through the hillside. Further on are bothies used for salmon fishing, which is still important in this part of the Tay. Beyond this are the ruins of Stanley House, where the mill owners lived in the 19th century. The land surrounding the ruins is still private property: please respect the owners' privacy.

THE TURBINE HOUSE

Electric lighting was installed at Stanley Mills in 1908. Machinery powered by electricity was to follow 14 years later. In 1921–2, a turbine house was

built on the peninsula – a circular concrete building with an ogee slate roof. Two Boving & Co. turbines were installed, and the existing lade was widened and extended.

The turbine house generated 1,100 horsepower and provided electricity for the mills, the street lighting and many of the houses in nearby Stanley village. It was only abandoned in 1965, when the mills were converted to mains electricity. In the 1990s, new turbines were installed in the building to generate electricity for the National Grid.

Above: The Stanley Mills complex seen from south of the Tay.

Left: The Turbine House, installed in 1921 to generate electricity from water power.

Opposite (far right): A photograph from 1917 shows residents on Store Street.

STANLEY VILLAGE

Built in the 1780s, the original Stanley village was a planned development to provide accommodation for the mill workers. It was laid out by James Stobie, factor to the Duke of Atholl.

Features to notice include Store Street, a brick tenement built in 1825; Stanley Church, built in 1828; Stanley St James Free Church, built in 1844; Stanley School, built on the west side of Duke Square in 1878; and the Tayside Hotel, which was a hostel for workers during and after the First and Second World Wars.

Once, most people in the village lived in company housing and many worked in the mills. Nowadays, most residents commute into Perth for work.

MANUFACTURING COTTON

Raw cotton is a downy fibre surrounding the seed pod of a tropical plant. It arrived at Stanley in bales and had to be disentangled, cleaned and blended before carding.

Carding is the process of combing cotton to straighten the fibres into a long rope called a sliver, which is fed into tall cans.

Drawing is the next stage, in which slivers are stretched into longer, straighter fibres.

Roving is carried out on a flyer frame. The fibre is drawn out yet again and slightly twisted, then wound onto a bobbin.

Spinning takes the yarn from the bobbins, stretches it and twists it onto a cop, a conical roll on a spindle, to make a finer thread.

If this yarn is to be woven into cloth, it has to undergo further processes.

Winding is the process of winding the yarn from cops onto bobbins. This produces weft to be attached to the weaver's shuttle.

Warping takes the same yarn and strengthens it by passing it through a solution of hot starch, a process known as dressing. This produced a smoother and stronger yarn, which could be used as warp (yarn stretched lengthwise on the loom) on power looms.

There were two types of spinning machinery to be found at Stanley in the early 1800s. The first was the water frame, patented by Richard Arkwright in 1769. This machine had two sets of leather rollers, the second revolving faster than the first and drawing out the yarn to the required thickness or count before

Top: A field of cotton.

Above left: A sliver of loosened cotton fibre taken from a carding machine.

Above: Cotton yarn on bobbins.

it was twisted. This yarn was strong enough to be used for the warp as well as the weft (the thread attached to the shuttle). In Scotland, water spinning was usually carried out by women and children.

The other spinning machine was the mule, invented by Samuel Crompton in 1779, which produced a finer yarn. This machine combined the leather rollers of the water frame with a moving carriage and spindles mounted on wheels, so that the thread was stretched and twisted as the carriage moved away from the rollers and wound onto the spindles when it moved back again. Mule spinning required greater strength than water spinning and was generally carried out by men.

Cotton weaving was initially carried out on handlooms and manual weaving continued on a large scale until the 1830s. However, from about 1810, the power loom began to be used in Scotland. Stanley had 60 power looms by June 1813.

Other processes introduced later at Stanley included bleaching: cleaning and whitening the cloth to improve its appearance and marketability.

'The first thing that hits you as soon as you walk into a cotton mill is the dust – and the smell.'

Derek Culbert, who worked at Stanley Mills in the 1950s and 1960s

Below: Detail from a 19th-century print showing the spinning room in a cotton factory.

THE STORY OF
STANLEY MILLS

'The Proprietor of a Situation where Mills may be erected, and a Power of Machinery worked ... calls the Attention of those Manufacturers, whose Business may require a great Command and Weight of Water, especially those concerned in the COTTON BRANCH'

Advertisement placed by the Duke of Atholl in the *Manchester Mercury*, 1785.

BEFORE STANLEY MILLS

By the late 18th century, British merchants had begun importing cotton, a 'new' fibre which was grown in India, the West Indies, South America and the southern states of the newly independent United States. Raw cotton was brought into Scotland via Glasgow, which had important trading links with North America and the Caribbean.

Meanwhile, in the North and Midlands of England, machines to prepare and spin cotton had been installed in purpose-built factories and driven by water power. This combination of international trade and rapid mechanisation drove the Industrial Revolution.

A textile industry had already sprung up in the area around Perth, where the River Tay and the River Almond provided water power and clean water for washing and bleaching. Until now, though, the industry had been based on linen, made from locally grown flax.

Perthshire now had a workforce skilled in textile production, and an ambitious merchant class with access to capital. The conditions were ripe for a cotton industry in the area.

Top: George Dempster, the local M.P., was one of seven partners who formed the original Stanley Company.

Above: William Sandeman, who owned a bleachworks at nearby Luncarty, was another founding member.

TIMELINE

1729

THE FIRST TUNNEL is dug through the hill at Stanley to provide water power for a corn mill.

1784

THE STANLEY COMPANY is formed by Richard Arkwright, George Dempster M.P. and five other partners.

23

THE EARLY YEARS: 1785-1823

Developments at Stanley were initiated by the local landowner John Murray, 4th Duke of Atholl.

In February 1785, he wrote, 'I have an Idea of establishing the Cotton Manufacture in this part of the World ... A great supply of water is necessary and no where in the Kingdom is there such a Command as at Stanley & by perforating the Hill I can bring in any quantity of the Tay I please.'

Another lobbyist for Stanley was George Dempster, the local M.P. On his journey back from Parliament, Dempster visited Cromford, Derbyshire, where the first water-powered cotton mill had been established in 1771. He met its owner, Richard Arkwright, and persuaded him to become involved at Stanley and at New Lanark.

The Stanley Company was formed with seven partners, who each invested £1,000 in the venture. The partners were Arkwright, Dempster, bleachworks owner William Sandeman, neighbouring landowner Robert Graham and three Perth merchants, including Andrew Keay, who, after training at Cromford, Derbyshire, became the first manager at Stanley.

Some 80 families were recruited from the Highlands as workers.

Above: A painting of Arkwright's first mill at Cromford, Derbyshire.

Left: The original contract between the seven founder members of the Stanley Company.

Below: John Murray, 4th Duke of Atholl, the local landowner who first saw the potential of Stanley as an industrial site.

This was at the time of the Clearances, when people were being evicted from the Atholl and Breadalbane estates in Highland Perthshire to make way for sheep farming. Between 40 and 50 Stanley workers were sent to Cromford for training in May 1785. By 1795, 350 people worked at Stanley Mills, of whom 300 were women and children under 16.

Arkwright withdrew from the venture as early as 1787, but the mills soon began to thrive. However, the French Wars of the 1790s brought an economic slump and, after the East Mill fire of 1799, Stanley Mills closed down. 'You would see the sky enlightened by the flames of our Stanley Flax Mill,' wrote George Dempster, who later claimed he had lost £8,000 (about £400,000 today) on the mills.

They were bought in 1801 by James Craig, a Glasgow muslin manufacturer, for £4,600. Craig was bankrolled by David Dale, the 'father' of the Scottish cotton industry and founder of New Lanark mills, and Stanley was supervised by his son-in-law, Robert Owen.

Owen bought raw cotton for Stanley on the Glasgow cotton exchange, gave advice to Craig on cotton manufacturing and arranged to have a water wheel made at New Lanark and shipped up to Stanley. In return, he and Dale received gifts of Tay salmon, which Owen described as 'quite fresh when it came'. However, the mills did not prosper and closed down again in 1813, with debts of over £40,000.

'I discovered in a romantic valley a palace of a most enormous size having, at least, a score of windows of a row, and five or six stories in height.'

George Dempster, M.P. for Perth, describing his first sight of Arkwright's Derbyshire mills.

Above: Robert Owen, who ran Stanley Mills in the early 19th century.

1787

THE BELL MILL opens and soon begins to flourish. The workforce reaches 350 within a decade.

1799

THE ORIGINAL EAST MILL burns down, leading to the temporary closure of Stanley Mills.

EXPANSION AND THE COTTON FAMINE: 1823-76

The mills were re-opened in 1823 by Buchanan & Co. of Glasgow, and an ambitious building programme began. The new owners installed a new lade system and expanded the East Mill. They also built the Mid Mill, the gas works, a church and a tenement for workers on Store Street. By 1831, the population of the village had risen to 2,000. Nearly half worked at the mills.

In 1833, Parliamentary Commissioners visited Stanley and other British textile mills to report on working conditions, particularly as they affected child workers. They reported that Stanley's workforce was largely composed of women and children or young adults. Of an 885-strong workforce, 540 were female and 497 were under 18. This was typical of the Scottish cotton industry at this time. Working hours were long – from 5.30am to 7pm, with 45 minutes for breakfast at 9am and the same for dinner at 2pm. Children finished work at 3.15pm to attend the company school.

Below: This photograph, taken during the Cotton Famine of the 1860s, shows the mills on the brink of closure.

Opposite (far right): Stanley Village Church, built by Buchanan & Co in 1828.

The youngest worker interviewed was Mary McGregor, aged 12, who had worked at Stanley for three years. She gave evidence, 'that she was not well at first and continues hoarse, but is otherwise well; that she likes the work and has no complaint to make; depones that she cannot write'. Reports like this led to the Factory Act of 1833, which prohibited the employment of children under nine in textile mills and restricted hours of work for 9–13-year-olds.

Two major events affected Stanley around this time. The first was the Disruption of 1843, when a schism in the Church of Scotland led to the formation of the Free Church of Scotland. The Buchanans had built the village church in 1828 and appointed its minister. As a result of the Disruption, most of the congregation left the company church and set up the Stanley Free Church, with its own school.

The second was the arrival of the railway in 1848. Prior to this, raw cotton had to be brought by cart from Glasgow, a ten-day return journey. Now it could be transferred in half a day.

In 1852, the Buchanans sold the mills to Samuel Howard, who became notorious during the Cotton Famine caused by the American Civil War (1861–5). He bought up large stocks of cotton, but instead of processing them at Stanley, he speculated in them, closing the mills down from 1862 to 1867, which caused great hardship.

'The traffic in our grass-grown streets are thinning, (A donkey on the verdure fondly browses), And none are left, alas! to do the spinning Except the spiders in the empty houses.'

John Campbell, 'A Voice from Stanley Mills', written in 1863, during the Cotton Famine.

1823

GEORGE BUCHANAN buys the mills, begins an ambitious expansion programme, and is instrumental in bringing the railway to Stanley.

1861–5

THE AMERICAN CIVIL WAR causes a Cotton Famine, which leads to a five-year closure at Stanley.

REVIVAL AND INNOVATION: 1876-1923

After Samuel Howard's death in 1872, the mills' fortunes were revived by Frank Stewart Sandeman, who took over in 1876 and bought the mills in 1880. Sandeman was unusual among Victorian industrialists as he had received a scientific education at Edinburgh University as well as the more usual practical training – in his case the Lancashire bleaching trade.

Although he liked to play the part of the country gentleman, Sandeman was an astute businessman and a great believer in scientific and technical education. In 1874 he had built the Manhattan Works in Dundee, a state-of-the-art jute mill.

At Stanley, he installed electric lighting in his house, replaced the water wheels with Gilkes turbines and introduced cotton belting as a staple of production. Belting was used to drive steam-powered machinery, and played a crucial role in the expansion of industry.

Below: The Stanley workforce in 1916.

Opposite (above right): An American advertisement from around 1918. Created by the English cartoonist George Studdy, Stanley the Caveman appeared in a series of promotional cartoons.

Opposite (below right): Frank Stewart Sandeman, who ran Stanley Mills from 1876, and bought the business in 1880.

It was introduced to Stanley by Perthshire-born William Fenton, who had worked in the Swedish cotton industry. Returning to Scotland in 1880, he leased part of Stanley Mills to produce belting. He was eventually bought out by Sandeman, who fully recognised the commercial importance of belting. The British Empire was at its height, and Stanley cotton belting was exported as far afield as India, South Africa, Australia and New Zealand.

However, the major activity at Stanley in the late 19th century was the spinning of selvedge cottons and sewing twines for the jute and linen industries of Dundee and Fife. A new department for bleaching and finishing cloth was also built.

During the First World War, the mills were kept busy producing webbing for the armed forces. Additional weavers were recruited from Fife and were housed in a hostel – the building is now the Tayside Hotel.

In 1916, Douglas Sandeman began to experiment with a light loom for weaving an 'endless' tape for cigarette manufacturing machinery and this also became a staple of production. These innovations helped Stanley Mills to survive the post-war Depression.

1880

COTTON BELTING is introduced at Stanley, soon becoming a mainstay of production.

1916

CIGARETTE TAPE emerges as another product crucial to the survival of the mills.

DECLINE AND CLOSURE: 1921-89

The years after the First World War were difficult times for the British textile industry. In the Dundee area, the various jute firms struggled to survive and came together in a conglomerate called Jute Industries. F.S. Sandeman & Co., which owned Manhattan Works in Dundee as well as Stanley Mills, joined this group in 1921.

Stanley survived, despite the worldwide Depression. Between 300 and 400 people were employed here and although there were periods of short-time working, the mills never closed. The firm continued to produce cotton yarn, bindings, webbings, tapes, conveyors and cotton belting.

From the mid-1930s, economic conditions improved. The firm supplied yarn to the Dundee jute trade and to Fife weaving firms. Stanley's weaving departments produced brake lining for cars, hosepipes, bookbinder webbing and chair webbing for upholstery.

The Second World War was a boom period for the Mills, which were kept busy manufacturing webbing for the armed forces. There was a labour shortage after the war and women workers were recruited from Italy and Germany.

India gained its independence in 1947, marking a major shift in Stanley's fortunes. The new Indian government imposed import tariffs on many cotton goods. This meant the loss of a major export market for Stanley.

'Cotton products like they manufactured in Stanley – the belting, the sailcloth – was in decline. I seen the writing on the wall in 1963. That's when my father left Stanley Mills.'

Derek Culbert, who worked at Stanley Mills in the 1950s and 1960s.

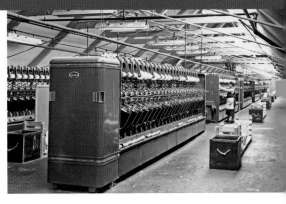

At the same time, the shift from steam-powered, belt-driven machinery to machines powered by electricity meant that the market for cotton belting was also shrinking rapidly. By 1967, the only cotton weaving left at Stanley was the cigarette tape section, but the firm still produced carpet yarn and industrial sewing yarn. The firm was also beginning to experiment with man-made acrylic fibres, which were used in the knitwear trade in the East Midlands.

In 1979 Bert Stott, the Mills' manager, led a management buyout. A new company was formed called Stanley Mills (Scotland), which concentrated on spinning acrylic yarn for knitwear. But the mills struggled to survive in a very competitive climate and eventually closed in 1989, after 200 years of textile manufacture.

After the closure, the site's condition deteriorated rapidly. In 1995, a fire gutted the North Range. In December 1995, the site was bought by Historic Scotland. Thanks to grants from the Heritage Lottery Fund and a collaboration with the Phoenix Trust – which has created 39 private residences in the East Mill and part of the Mid Mill – it has been possible to restore Stanley Mills to its present condition.

Top: Spinning machines in the Mid Mill in 1960.

Above: Bert Stott, manager of Stanley Mills, in 1960. He went on to lead the management buy-out of 1979.

Opposite: Webbing – cotton fabric to hold equipment – was produced at Stanley Mills for British troops during both World Wars.

1921	1979

TURBINES INSTALLED in a new building on the Stanley peninsula, generating electricity to power the machines.

MANAGEMENT BUY-OUT to form Stanley Mills (Scotland) Ltd, but by 1989 closure becomes inevitable.

Stanley Mills is one of 20 Historic Scotland sites in Perthshire, a selection of which is shown below.

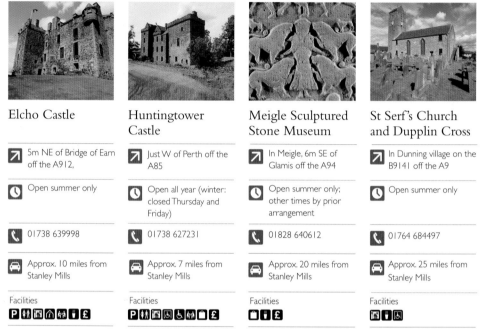

Elcho Castle

↗ 5m NE of Bridge of Earn off the A912,

🕐 Open summer only

📞 01738 639998

🚗 Approx. 10 miles from Stanley Mills

Facilities
🅿️ 🚻 🖼️ 🏠 🚼 🚽 £

Huntingtower Castle

↗ Just W of Perth off the A85

🕐 Open all year (winter: closed Thursday and Friday)

📞 01738 627231

🚗 Approx. 7 miles from Stanley Mills

Facilities
🅿️ 🚻 🖼️ 🖼️ ♿ 🚼 🛍️ £

Meigle Sculptured Stone Museum

↗ In Meigle, 6m SE of Glamis off the A94

🕐 Open summer only; other times by prior arrangement

📞 01828 640612

🚗 Approx. 20 miles from Stanley Mills

Facilities
🖼️ 🚽 £

St Serf's Church and Dupplin Cross

↗ In Dunning village on the B9141 off the A9

🕐 Open summer only

📞 01764 684497

🚗 Approx. 25 miles from Stanley Mills

Facilities
🖼️ 🚽 🖼️

For more information on all Historic Scotland sites, visit **www.historic-scotland.gov.uk**
To order tickets and a wide range of gifts, visit **www.historic-scotland.gov.uk/shop**

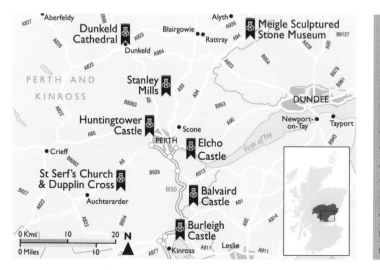

Key to facilities	
Admission charge	£
Bus/coach parking	🅿️
Car parking	🅿️
Interpretive display	🖼️
Picnic area	🚼
Reasonable wheelchair access	♿
Shop	🛍️
Cafe/restaurant	☕
Tea/coffee stop	🥤
Toilets	🚻
Visitor centre	🏠
Disabled toilets	♿
Bicycle parking	🚲